I0626959

Riverview

A Monument to Greek
Revival Architecture

Patricia Shannon Evans

TIBBEE TALES
PUBLISHING

Published by Tibbee Tales Publishing

Columbus, MS 39705

All illustrations are from the author's collection and the collection of the Billups-Garth Archives at the Columbus-Lowndes Public Library except where noted.

First published in 2025

Manufactured in the United States

979 8 993 1019-10

Evans, Patricia Shannon

Riverview: A Monument to Greek Revival Architecture/Patricia Shannon Evans.

p.cm.

Includes bibliographical references

979 8 993 1019-10

1. Architecture–James Lull (MS)--History 2. Architecture–Greek Revival (MS) 3. Antebellum South–Columbus, MS (MS and AL) 4. Charles McLaran–Planter (MS) 5. Charles McLaran–Financier and Businessman (MS and MO) 6. Mississippi–Civil War Era (MS) 7. John Gilmer-Businessman and Plantation Owner

Historical Silences in Research

As you turn these pages, you may notice the stories of the enslaved Black men, women, and children who once lived and labored here are not fully told. That absence is not because their lives were unimportant, but because their voices were deliberately silenced by history.

Many were recorded only as numbers or listed as property. Their names were left out. Their experiences were ignored. Their humanity was denied, both in their time and in the records that followed.

As modern historians, we wish we could tell you who they were, what they felt, how they lived, and what they dreamed of. But those details were rarely written down. That silence is real, and it carries deep weight.

Still, this book serves as a reminder that they were here. Their hands built these homes. Their presence shaped this place. Their lives mattered.

Though I cannot share every name or story, I hope this work encourages others to keep searching, asking, and honoring the lives that history tried to erase. To the ones I couldn't fully name, please know, you are seen, you are remembered, and you will not be forgotten.

Acknowledgements

I would like to express my deepest gratitude to my "family" for their unwavering support throughout this journey. To Himself, who endured late nights and countless revisions with a smile, and to my fellow childhood friend and editor Kate Doster Wright, who inspired me with her boundless imagination.

A special thanks to my cousin Billy Cox, for believing in this project and championing it tirelessly. The entire archive team at the Lowndes County Library (especially Mona Vance-Ali) deserves applause for their insightful feedback, support, and dedication to shaping this project.

Heartfelt thanks to my writing accountability pal, author Julie Liddell Whitehead, whose constructive criticism and constant encouragement kicked my backside when needed. Special thanks to my dear sweet friend Rachel Baskerville George who keeps me on track and keeps me digging into Columbus history to answer all manner of questions.

This book would not be the same without the exceptional cover design by Paxton Garrard. His creativity brought the story to life. My marketing lead in all of this is Andrew "AJ" Woody. His insights and hard work are greatly appreciated. I love my team and all they have done to support me on this project and how they pushed me over the finish line.

Finally, to the readers who love history, thank you for giving these homes and our beautiful town a place in your heart.

A Monument to Greek Revival Architecture

In the late 1840s, as steamboats plied the waters of the Tombigbee River in Mississippi, an ambitious project took shape on Pleasant Ridge. A magnificent mansion was slowly emerging from the red clay soil of Columbus. This was Riverview, destined to become one of the finest examples of Greek Revival architecture in the American South.

Riverview is one of the finest examples of Greek Revival architecture in the American South. Built between 1847 and 1853 in Columbus, Mississippi, this magnificent mansion showcases the wealth and architectural ambitions of the antebellum period. The estate represents the culmination of these classic design principles and exemplifies the sophisticated architectural tastes of wealthy Southern planters before the Civil War. Like many grand homes of this era, Riverview's design made a bold statement about its owners' prosperity, education, and refinement.

Construction began in 1847, during a time when America was embracing classical architecture with passionate enthusiasm. With quarter-inch precision - a feat that would impress even modern craftsmen the builders crafted and laid over a million bricks. The mansion's twin faces, identical in their grandeur, gazed both toward the bustling town and across the rolling river.

Four massive columns rose on each side, supporting porticos that seemed to touch the sky. These weren't just any columns – crafted from carefully selected old-growth cypress trees, each column reaching thirty feet into the air and measuring three feet around. The builders, both free and enslaved, worked tirelessly to create perfect symmetry and balance in every detail.

Perhaps most striking was Riverview's innovative design for natural lighting. Crowning the mansion was a twelve-foot square cupola - a tower of glass and architectural artistry. Its windows weren't just for show; the architect placed each one to paint the interior with colored light throughout the day. As the sun moved across the sky, red, cobalt, green, and amethyst hues danced through the stairwell, creating an ever-changing display of natural artistry.

Inside, Riverview was a marvel of refinement and innovation. The main hall stretched broad and welcoming; its sixteen-foot ceilings adorned with intricate plasterwork that would have impressed European aristocrats. A magnificent mahogany staircase spiraled upward, its unusual scroll-like newel post catching the eye of every visitor.

The double parlors were where the real magic happened. Here, black marble fireplaces imported from Italy provided elegant focal points, while gilded mirrors and brass chandeliers reflected the warm glow of evening gatherings. In a clever bit of engineering, a vast (or keep huge and just put a comma behind it) wooden panel between the dining rooms could be raised into the ceiling, transforming separate spaces into a grand banquet hall.

When Riverview debuted in November 1852, it caused such a sensation that the local newspaper, The Southern Standard, devoted extensive coverage to its unveiling. They described not just a house but a self-contained estate occupying an entire city block, surrounded by "luxuriant native forest trees" and protected by an ornamental cast-iron fence.

Today, while the property is smaller than its original expanse, Riverview stands as remarkably intact as it was in 1852. The same cast-iron lions still guard its entrance, the same marble floors still catch the morning light, and the same stunning cupola still crowns its heights. It serves as both a testament to architectural ambition and a window into a fascinating period of American history.

Riverview tells us much more than just an architectural story. It speaks of a time when wealthy planters-built townhouses to escape plantation isolation, when architectural pattern books spread sophisticated designs across the growing nation, and when craftsmanship was measured in quarter-inch perfection. Its walls have witnessed countless celebrations, survived a civil war, and weathered nearly two centuries of Southern summers.

In every carved detail and carefully laid brick, Riverview reminds us that buildings can be more than just shelter - they can be works of art that survive their creators to tell stories to future generations.

The mansion reflects the antebellum South's economic prosperity and social aspirations. Its design drew heavily from pattern books that spread classical architectural ideas across America. The house remains an invaluable resource for understanding 19th-century building techniques, social customs, and architectural development.

Riverview - The Vision Begins

The story of Columbus begins with Native American roots, where Chickasaw and Choctaw peoples called the area "Possum Town" because one of the original settlers, Spirus Roach was described by the Choctaw as resembling a possum. Prior to Roach's time, in 1540, Spanish explorer Hernando de Soto became the first European to document this lush region while searching for the legendary city of gold, El Dorado. The area remained largely untouched by European settlers until the late 1700s when William Cooper established a trading post.

In 1817, a pivotal moment occurred when a small log cabin was built near what would become downtown Columbus. The settlement grew slowly until 1819-1820, when the U.S. Army constructed a "Military Road" connecting New Orleans to Nashville, passing through the heart of the future city. In 1821, the settlement was officially chartered as Columbus, leaving behind its "Possum Town" nickname.

Formally founded in 1821, Columbus became a strategic location due to its position on the Tombigbee River bluffs. It had access to fertile Black Belt Prairie soil and was the third-largest river port in Mississippi. It also was on Andrew Jackson's Military Road.

The 1820s brought significant developments, including the arrival of the first steamboat, the Cotton Plant, in 1822. Education also took root with the establishment of Franklin Academy, the state's first public school. The period from 1835 to 1860 marked Columbus's Golden Age. The rich Black Prairie soil attracted wealthy planters from the East Coast, who built grand mansions throughout the city. By the 1850s, Columbus was booming with a population of 3,500 filled with churches, schools, and thriving businesses including 37 manufacturing establishments.

The 1830s and 40s brought unprecedented change to Mississippi. Where Native American tribes once lived, vast cotton plantations now stretched across the fertile Black Belt soil. The state's population exploded nearly 200% as settlers poured sought fortune in the cotton boom.

Columbus exemplified this transformation. From a frontier trading post of just 2,000 people in 1830, it grew into a sophisticated town of over 8,000 by 1850. Its location on the Tombigbee River made it ideal for shipping cotton to Mobile and New Orleans. Elegant hotels, churches, and academies lined the streets. The sound of hammers echoed as fine homes rose on every hill.

The 1830s marked a transformative period in Mississippi's history. Following treaties with the Choctaw and Chickasaw nations, over 20 million acres became available for settlement. This led to a 175% population increase between 1830-1840 and a 197% increase in the enslaved population. Total population growth in Mississippi jumped from 136,621 to 791,305 between 1830-1860.

In the warm spring of 1847, Colonel Charles McLaran stood on a hill overlooking the bustling river town of Columbus, Mississippi. The successful cotton planter and businessman had a vision - to build the grandest home north of Natchez. As steamboats churned past on the

Tombigbee River below, McLaran could already see in his mind the majestic columns and sweeping verandas of his future mansion.

The site he chose was perfect - a commanding hilltop with views extending for miles across the river valley. The location would catch cooling breezes in summer and allow the mansion to be seen from approaching riverboats, making it a landmark of wealth and refinement.

McLaran spared no expense in creating his masterpiece. He hired James S. Lull, a talented architect from Vermont known for his classical designs.

James Lull: Visionary Eclectic Architect of Riverview

In the rich architectural tapestry of Columbus, Mississippi, few buildings showcase the mastery of James Lull quite like the magnificent Riverview mansion. This architectural masterpiece is a testament to Lull's innovative design approach and attention to detail. The mansion's enduring presence on the landscape has influenced generations of architects and historians, making it a cornerstone of Southern architectural heritage. As workers began laying the hand-cut limestone foundation blocks, few could have imagined how this 14,000-square-foot building would come to represent the pinnacle of Southern architectural achievement and survive nearly two centuries of American history.

Born in Windsor, Vermont in the early 1808, James Lull brought his architectural expertise to Columbus, Mississippi, by 1839. His formal education in Philadelphia equipped him with a deep understanding of classical architectural styles, particularly Greek Revival, which he would later introduce to Columbus. Lull's training under renowned Philadelphia architects exposed him to advanced construction techniques of the period, classical proportional systems, contemporary innovations in building materials, and the emerging American interpretation of European styles.

Lull studied under renowned Philadelphia architect William Strickland and arrived in Columbus in 1835, he had already begun transforming the city's architectural landscape with his innovative designs. His formal training in Philadelphia, and his New England sensibilities and appreciation for Southern climate needs, created a unique architectural perspective that would revolutionize Columbus's built environment.

Initial planning of Riverview began in 1843 with extensive site surveys. In the warm Mississippi sunlight of 1844, the ground was broken for what would become one of Columbus's most magnificent homes - the Riverview mansion. Construction started using locally sourced materials, and over 100 skilled craftsmen working for three years. It cost approximately $50,000 (equivalent to $1.7 million today).

James Lull stood at the construction site; his architectural plans rolled carefully under his arm. As workers began laying the foundation, few could have imagined how this building would come to represent the pinnacle of Southern architectural achievement.

The story of Riverview began with Colonel Charles McLaran, a wealthy cotton merchant who amassed a fortune of over $2 million (equivalent to roughly $70 million today), dreamed of a home that would reflect his success and status. McLaran commissioned James Lull to create a home that reflected his success and status. McLaran gave Lull an unprecedented budget of $85,000 - an astronomical sum for the 1840s. He chose James Lull, who had already made a name for himself by introducing Greek Revival architecture to Columbus. Riverview was designed as a twin to Camelia Place (Lull's own home) and exemplified this style with unique "Columbus Eclectic" elements.

As Riverview rose from the Mississippi soil, it became clear that this was more than just another plantation house. It was a symbol of the antebellum South's prosperity and architectural sophistication. Its twin relationship with Lull's own home, Camelia Place, created a unique architectural dialogue that still fascinates historians today.

Lull wasn't content with simply copying classical designs. Lull's genius innovative designs for Riverview included a unique ventilation system, advanced load-bearing techniques, deep porches, and a raised basement for air circulation. He developed what became known as the "Columbus Eclectic" style, blending Greek Revival grandeur with Gothic and Italianate elements. The result was uniquely American yet deeply rooted in European architectural traditions. Lull developed what became known as the "Columbus Eclectic" style, characterized by:

- Greek Revival elements: 30-foot Ionic columns, symmetrical façade, entablature details
- Gothic influences: Pointed arch windows in the upper story, trefoil decorative elements

- Italianate features: Wide eaves with decorative brackets, cupola, curved marble stairs.

The construction was a massive undertaking. Over one hundred skilled craftsmen worked tirelessly for three years, their tools ringing across the property as they shaped local materials into architectural poetry. Every detail was meticulously planned and executed, from the soaring thirty-foot Ionic columns to the intricate egg-and-dart molding that would crown the cornices.

The construction was a massive undertaking spanning three years (1844-1847). It required over 100 skilled craftsmen, including master stonemasons from Italy, 30 enslaved laborers who manufactured the bricks on-site, 12 master carpenters from New England, and three master plasterers from Philadelphia.

Materials used included:

- 750,000 locally made bricks
- 200 tons of marble from Tennessee
- 85,000 board feet of heart pine lumber
- 15,000 square feet of cypress shingles
- Hand-carved limestone capitals

- Double-hung sash windows with 12-over-12 panes
- Detailed cornices featuring egg-and-dart molding
- Wraparound veranda with intricate ironwork
- Symmetrical chimneys with decorative caps
- Curved front steps made from Tennessee marble

The interior was equally impressive. Fourteen-foot ceilings created airy spaces filled with natural light from twelve-over-twelve-pane windows. Heart pine floors echoed with the footsteps of craftsmen as they installed eight unique marble fireplaces and carved elaborate black walnut staircases. The interior showcased unprecedented luxury. There were eight unique marble fireplaces, with unique marble mantels, each from a different quarry. It has 24 rooms, including a 40' × double parlors' ballroom. The hand-carved Black walnut staircases with intricate spiral newel posts floats from the foyer to the cupola. The house has custom-made brass hardware from Philadelphia, hand-painted French wallpaper depicting classical scenes, and gas lighting fixtures (revolutionary for the time).

There are 14-foot ceilings throughout the main floor, original heart pine flooring, elaborate plaster medallions in the main parlors, and period-specific crown molding and baseboards.

Riverview survived the Civil War and has continued to endure generations of change. Today, it remains a testament to James Lull's genius and the craftsmanship of those who built it. Listed on the National Register of Historic Places, it showcases Lull's innovative architectural approach representing the prosperity of pre-Civil War Columbus. It remains largely intact, preserving the historical authenticity of the building.

When James Lull died in 1871, he left behind more than just buildings - he left a legacy of architectural innovation that transformed Columbus. Riverview is perhaps his greatest achievement, a masterpiece that continues to inspire and educate nearly two centuries after its construction began. His designs established new standards for residential architecture in the South, introduced innovative construction methods, and influenced subsequent building designs throughout Mississippi.

Standing before Riverview today, visitors can still feel the power of Lull's vision. In every careful detail, from the curved Tennessee marble steps to the blown glass cabinet doors, we see the work of a master architect who understood that great buildings do more than shelter - they tell stories that echo through time.

Riverview represents more than just a beautiful antebellum home - it embodies the architectural genius of James Lull and stands as a living museum of 19th-century craftsmanship and design. Its twin relationship with Camelia Place and its pristine preservation makes it an invaluable piece of American architectural history. Its meticulous documentation, preservation, and ongoing influence make it an invaluable resource for understanding architectural history and Southern culture.

The mansion debuted in November 1852, an event that received extensive coverage in the local newspaper. The *Southern Standard* provided a contemporary description of Colonel McLaran's new residence:

> *It includes an entire square in the plan of the city, bordering on the bank of the Tombigbee river on one side, and is*

enclosed by a neat pilastered brick wall about five feet in height, except/he entire front and a small space in the centre (sic) of the rear, where a highly ornamental castiron paling supplies its place, and gives an air to the premises alike tasteful and imposing. The building occupies a central position in the square, surounded by luxurient (sic) native forest trees, and is a solid quadrangular figure, of the Corinthian or composite order, constructed of the finest compressed brick, wrought into pilastered walls, covering an area sixty one feet square, and rising forty feet in height from the base to the eaves,-surmounted by an observatory, twenty feel square, and towering up to an elevation of sixty feet above the ground. the spacious windows of which-three on each side-by the cunning contrivance of the artist, present to the eye of the observer from within, the appearance in the surrounding objects of the four seasons, viz. Winter, Spring, Summer and Fall. Two spacious porticos placed exactly opposite, the one in front, and the other in the rear, each supported by four insulated anlae (sic), standing in rows parallel with the walls of the building, and rising from marble plinths up to the eaves of the main structure, with pavements composed of the most exquisite marble mosaic work-complete the outlines of this stately private residence.

Among the most striking ornamental objects to be seen about the exterior of the establishment are two emblems of fidelity, chiseled out of white marble in half salient attitudes, and placed upon the projecting buttresses on each side of the steps of the front entrance- welcoming the visitor to the quiet single blessedness, and the liberal hospitality of the owner; and two huge recumbent cast-iron lions, occupying similar positions in the rear, and symbolically guarding the opposite door and back premises. We can present only a mere glance at the various apartments, and many other splendid objects, connected with the internal structure, and the exquisite style and finish of everything in this admirable mansion. Pilaster walled parlors, adorned with the richest entablatures,- spacious party saloons, and private boudoirs,- mant/es (sic) of the purest Egyptian marble, -ceilings of the most lofty elevation, the richest plaster panel work, and the most superb finish, -an admirably contrived and elaborately executed *mahogany spiral stainvay-a chef d'ouvre (sic) in this art- starting from the centre of the building on the first floor, and terminating at the observatory-comprise a few of the most striking objects which present themselves on all sides, and each, and all alike attract our lively attention, and captivate the taste of the beholder.*

The Southern Standard, Columbus, Mississippi, November 27, 1852.

An American Success Story: Charles McLaran of Riverview & the Rise of a Business Titan

In the bustling port city of Baltimore in 1823, a young man named Charles McLaran dreamed of making his mark on the world. Growing up in a modest merchant family, he learned the basics of commerce by helping in his father's small hardware store on the waterfront. At twenty-one, with only $78 in savings, a leather-bound ledger book, and unwavering determination, he bid farewell to his Maryland home and headed south to Birmingham, Alabama. This 750-mile journey, primarily by stagecoach and riverboat, would set in motion a series of events that would shape not only his destiny but also the development of several American cities.

McLaran's first year in Birmingham tested his resolve. He worked 16-hour days as a clerk in Henderson's General Store, sleeping in the back room and saving every penny. He existed on cornbread and beans. At night he taught himself cotton grading and learning the complexities of the cotton futures market. His breakthrough came when his uncle passed away, leaving him an unexpected inheritance of $3,000 (equivalent to roughly $95,000 today).

McLaran's inheritance provided him with capital to invest. It also allowed him to purchase his first 120-acre plantation for $800 and invest $1200 in essential equipment. He built a small cotton gin and reserved his remaining working capital for expansion. Displaying the business acumen that would become his trademark, he entered the lucrative cotton industry. The antebellum South's economy revolved around "white gold," and McLaran's strategic purchase of three plantations along the Black Warrior River proved to be a shrewd investment. By 1840, his operations employed over 200 workers and produced 1,500 bales annually.

By 1847, McLaran had established himself as a respected businessman in Columbus. He was a Mason and a major contributor to First Baptist

Church in 1838. His contribution provided the funding for the congregation's first church, a James Lull design.

His greatest achievement during this period was co-founding what would later become the First National Bank of Columbus, investing $25,000 of his capital. As its first president, he introduced innovative lending practices for small farmers and established the first mortgage department in the region. He also created a revolutionary system for tracking customer credit. Some of his lending practices were groundbreaking for that time. He introduced seasonal payment schedules aligned with harvest times. He created collateral-based loans using farm equipment and character-based credit assessments. He also offered flexible interest rates based on crop futures. He extended banking hours during harvest season and hired mobile banking agents who visited rural communities. He also hosted financial literacy workshops and bilingual services for the burgeoning local German immigrant population.

As the bank's first president, he demonstrated leadership abilities that caught the attention of political operatives who repeatedly urged him to run for governor—offers he consistently declined.

McLaran joined the local Masonic order in 1848, advancing to the distinguished Royal Arch degree. His weekly Masonic meetings became crucial networking opportunities connecting him with other prominent businessmen, including Governor John Matthews, railroad magnate William Roundtree, and cotton broker James Pemberton.

As storm clouds of civil war gathered on the horizon, McLaran strategically decided to sell Riverview to John Gilmer in 1857. McLaran relocated to St. Louis. Rather than merely focusing on personal profit, he dedicated himself to civic improvement.

His most notable contribution was helping establish the metropolitan police system (1857) and one of the first police commissioners. He founded St. Louis' first public library in 1859 and created the city's first fire insurance company in 1860. He also served on the St. Louis Board of Education from 1861-1865 and personally funded three rural schoolhouses. He created a scholarship program for orphaned children and was a large financial supporter of teacher training programs.

McLaran helped modernize St. Louis by financing the city's first steam-powered fire engine. He contributed to the city's street paving program projects and the municipal water system. He advocated for public transportation in and around the city as well.

In 1867, McLaran partnered with his nephew to establish McLaran & Williams, a wholesale hardware business. Through strategic planning and excellent management, their company became one of the largest hardware enterprises in the Western United States. They revolutionized the industry by introducing mail-order catalogs, creating a regional distribution network of 12 warehouses, implementing standardized pricing across territories, and offering credit to established merchants. Their company partnered with three railroad companies and developed a river barge delivery system for their goods.

They created a 200-page illustrated catalog of their goods and services and offered a 30-day guarantee on every item. They offered credit terms for established merchants and were famous for their seasonal sales promotions. McLaran's influence extended beyond business. He established technical training programs and created over 1,000 jobs.

From McLaran's 1870 speech to the St. Louis Chamber of Commerce:

> *"Commerce without conscience is merely greed dressed in fine clothes. Our duty as businessmen extends beyond our ledgers to the very heart of our communities. We must build not just wealth but institutions that serve the public good."*

After eight successful years leading McLaran & Williams, Charles McLaran retired from active business operations. He spent his remaining years managing his substantial estate, a testament to his business acumen and diverse investments.

The Champion of Women's Rights: Colonel John Gilmer's Story

Colonel John Gilmer was born in Georgia in 1792, during George Washington's presidency. He became not just a wealthy planter but also a progressive lawmaker who changed the lives of women in Mississippi forever.

As a young man of 22, John married his first love, Lucy Thornton Johnson, in a ceremony typical of the Georgia planter class. Together, they built a life in Georgia, where John proved himself an ambitious and successful planter, cultivating primarily cotton and tobacco. Their family included six children: William, Mary, Elizabeth, John Jr., Thomas, and Sarah. Their growing number of enslaved laborers reflected their prosperity - a common but troubling measure of wealth in the antebellum South. By 1825, Gilmer's plantation had grown to over 1,000 acres.

After Lucy's death from yellow fever around 1830, John married Susannah Crawford Barnett Gresham, a wealthy widow who brought considerable assets to the marriage, including several hundred acres of prime Georgia farmland. This marriage began a new chapter in his life and likely influenced his later views on women's property rights. By 1835, John moved his growing family to Mississippi, settling near Columbus in Lowndes County, where rich soil and expanding cotton markets promised new opportunities.

What made Colonel Gilmer truly remarkable was his forward-thinking approach to women's rights. In 1839, he authored and championed what became known as the "Woman's Law" in Mississippi. This groundbreaking legislation was revolutionary for its time - it allowed married women to own property separately from their husbands. Under this law, a wife's property couldn't be seized for her husband's debts or sold without her consent.

John Gilmer's groundbreaking analysis of the Mississippi Married Women's Property Act of 1839 transformed our understanding of this landmark legislation. While previous scholars focused primarily on gender equality and economic reforms, Gilmer revealed crucial connections to Native American tribal law, particularly the Chickasaw nation's influence.

His work earned recognition because it:

- Introduced previously overlooked Native American perspectives
- Connected multiple historical threads into a cohesive narrative
- Challenged traditional interpretations of the law's origins

Gilmer's main contribution was his analysis of the Chickasaw tribal law connection to the Mississippi Married Women's Property Act of 1839. He identified key economic pressures that created the growing demand for cotton plantation land, the banking and credit practices of the 1830s, the impact of the Panic of 1837 and the role of land speculation in territorial expansion. He provided a unique perspective that went beyond just social and economic factors.

Gilmer argued two main points:

1. He connected the Hadley family to the Fisher v. Allen court case by suggesting there were

ulterior motives behind passing the bill. Gilmer meticulously documented how the Hadley family's involvement in Fisher v. Allen (1837) went beyond simple property rights:

- Revealed business connections between Hadley family members and land speculators
- Traced financial records showing interest in tribal land acquisition
- Demonstrated how family members lobbied for the Act's passage

2. Gilmer's research showed that the Act served multiple purposes:

- Enabled Chickasaw and Choctaw women to sell tribal lands independently
- Created a larger pool of potential sellers in the land market
- Accelerated the transfer of Native American lands to white settlers
- Aligned with federal policies promoting western expansion

He proposed that the Act would make it easier for tribal lands to be sold to white settlers if both Chickasaw and Choctaw women (not just men) could sell property.

Gilmer illuminated how different legal systems –
traditional Chickasaw property rights, the federal
Indian removal policies, Mississippi state
property laws, English Common Law traditions,
and women's property rights in the 1830s –
interacted.

Some of the key provisions of the Woman's Law
were that women could own slaves, livestock,
and land independently. Married women could
maintain separate bank accounts, and the
property she brought into marriage remained
under her control. It allowed women could write
wills and inherit property and provided protection
of women's property from their husbands'
creditors.

Gilmer's work is significant because he revealed
previously unexplored Native American
influences on the law. He identified potential
political and economic motivations behind the
Act's passage. His research added depth to
understanding why Mississippi became the first
state to pass such legislation. Gilmer's work
revolutionized the field by introducing
interdisciplinary analysis methods and
challenging single-cause explanations. He
encouraged research helped explain why
Mississippi led other states in women's property

rights, how Native American practices influenced state law, and the complex motivations behind seemingly progressive legislation.

Gilmer's work continues to influence modern legal history research methods. It also continues to inform the understanding of women's property rights evolution and the intersection between law and economic policy. The principles established by Gilmer's law would later influence The Married Women's Property Acts of the 1850s, the early suffragist movements, modern community property

Colonel Gilmer's influence extended far beyond lawmaking. Gilmer purchased Riverview from Charles McLaran in 1857 so his wife and children could live in town in the winter months to attend church and school. He became one of the area's most successful businessmen, helping to build the Gilmer Hotel, a three-story brick edifice that became Columbus's social center. He developed what became known as the Gilmer Road, a vital transportation route connecting Columbus to important trade centers.

Those who knew him described Gilmer as a man of simple manners and frugal habits despite his wealth. He wore plain clothing, preferred substance over style, and was known to quote extensively from Shakespeare and the Bible. He had a sharp intellect and maintained an extensive library, particularly favoring works about politics, religion, and philosophy. His brother James wrote that he was "clear-headed, sharp-witted, and attentive to his interests, yet always fair in his dealings."

Beyond his famous Woman's Law, Gilmer advocated for other progressive causes. He supported the establishment of Franklin Academy, one of Mississippi's first public schools. He advocated for better treatment of slaves (though remaining a slaveholder himself) and promoted agricultural innovation and crop diversification. He also supported the development of local churches and community centers.

When Colonel Gilmer died in 1860, on the eve of the Civil War, he left behind a significant legacy. His will reflected his lifelong respect for women's rights - he named his wife Susan as the sole executor of his estate, an unusual move for the time. She was an independently wealthy woman after his death and remained in the home until her death in 1881. He ensured his daughters received equal inheritances with his sons and established trust funds for his grandchildren's education, regardless of gender.

Gilmer's Hotel: A Columbus Landmark

In the early 19th century, a small plot of land in Columbus, Mississippi, began its journey to becoming a landmark. The year was 1819, and Gideon Lincecum, a pioneer and naturalist, had just built the town's first frame house on what would later be known as the Gilmer block. This modest structure, likely made of locally sourced timber, stood as a testament to the burgeoning settlement. Lincecum's choice of location was no accident; situated at the intersection of two major thoroughfares, it was prime real estate in the young town.

By the 1830s, the corner of the block boasted the Eagle Hotel, a testament to the growing town's need for accommodations. As Columbus flourished, so did the Eagle, becoming a hub of activity and a witness to the town's transformation. With its simple yet sturdy construction, the hotel offered travelers a place to rest their heads and swap stories. Many a deal was struck, and friendships forged over hearty meals and strong drinks.

In 1860, a visionary named John Gilmer saw potential in the aging Eagle Hotel site. He began construction on a grand, four-story brick building that would become the Gilmer Hotel. Gilmer's ambition was to create an establishment that would rival the finest hotels in the South. The plans called for ornate ironwork balconies, spacious dining rooms, and luxurious furnishings. However, fate had other plans for the unfinished structure.

As the Civil War erupted, the incomplete Gilmer found an unexpected purpose. In April 1862, following the bloody Battle of Shiloh, the hotel's unfinished rooms became a sanctuary for wounded soldiers. Its walls, though bare, sheltered nearly 800 injured men, far exceeding its intended capacity of 450 beds. The sounds of hammers and saws were replaced by the groans of the wounded and the hurried footsteps of nurses and doctors. The Gilmer, still in its infancy, had already become a crucial part of Columbus's history.

After the war, the Gilmer rose from the ashes of conflict. The builders returned and completed the first three floors, and the hotel opened its doors as the Gilmer House. It quickly became the social heart of Columbus, hosting gatherings and welcoming travelers from far and wide. The hotel's ballroom became the scene of elaborate parties, where the elite of Columbus society would dance the night away. The dining room served southern delicacies, earning a reputation for its fried chicken and pecan pie that spread far beyond the city limits.

By 1907, the Gilmer was showing its age. A major renovation breathed new life into the old hotel. The completion of the fourth floor added much-needed space for guests. They installed modern amenities like hot and cold running water, steam heat, and an electric elevator. These improvements were cutting-edge for their time, especially in a small Southern town. The Gilmer was ready to face the 20th century in style, its newly refurbished rooms blending traditional Southern charm and modern convenience.

Over the years, the Gilmer played hosted a parade of notable guests. Will Rogers, the famous humorist, is said to have remarked that the Gilmer's hospitality was "as warm as a Mississippi summer." Jack Dempsey, the heavyweight boxing champion, stayed at the Gilmer while on a tour of the South. Hollywood royalty also graced its halls; Clark Gable reportedly charmed the staff during his stay, while Bob Hope cracked jokes in the lobby. Doris Day, the beloved singer and actress, is rumored to have sung an impromptu performance in the hotel's dining room, much to the delight of other guests.

In 1962, after a century of service, the Gilmer Hotel was razed to make way for a modern Downtowner Motor Inn. The demolition marked the end of an era, but the memories and stories of the Gilmer lived on in the hearts of Columbus residents. Many locals protested the decision, seeing it as a loss of a piece of their history. The wrecking ball that brought down the Gilmer also seemed to herald the end of a certain kind of Southern gentility and charm that the old hotel had embodied.

Today, as the now run-down motel faces its uncertain future, the story of the Gilmer Hotel serves as a poignant reminder of the ever-changing face of a city. From its origins as a simple tavern to its glory days as a grand hotel, the Gilmer block has been a silent witness to the ebb and flow of Columbus's history.

The Gilmer's legacy extends beyond its physical presence. It represents a microcosm of American history, from the pioneering spirit of its early days to the trauma of the Civil War, from the elegance of the Gilded Age to the modernization of the early 20th century. The hotel's story intertwines with the larger narrative of Columbus and the South, reflecting the region's triumphs and challenges.

Local historians have worked to preserve the memories associated with the Gilmer. Oral histories have been collected from former staff and guests, painting a vivid picture of life in and around the hotel. These stories, filled with laughter, tears, and nostalgia, keep the spirit of the Gilmer alive.

Though the building may be gone, its legacy endures, a testament to the rich tapestry of stories that make up the fabric of a community. The Gilmer Hotel, in its various incarnations, served as more than just a place to sleep; it was a gathering place, a landmark, and a symbol of Columbus itself. Its story reminds us of the importance of preserving our historical landmarks, not just for their architectural value but for the memories and shared experiences they represent.

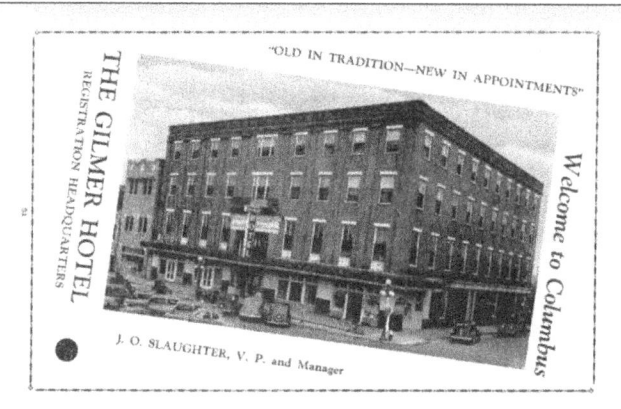

The Gilmer Hotel thrived long into the 20th Century

A streetcar briefly operated on Main Street in Columbus.

A Confederate Captain's Story: William Washington Humphries

In the sweltering summer of 1841, as cotton fields stretched across the Mississippi landscape, a boy was born who would later become a notable figure in military and political circles of the American South. William Washington Humphries entered the world on June 20th in Columbus, Mississippi, born to Dr. William Washington Humphries Sr. and Martha Elizabeth Gregory. The Humphries family was well-established in the community, with Dr. Humphries running a successful medical practice that served wealthy planters and common townspeople alike.

Young William showed exceptional promise in his academic pursuits from an early age. He excelled in rhetoric and mathematics at the Columbus Male Academy, where teachers noted his natural leadership abilities and sharp intellect. By seventeen, he had earned admission to the prestigious University of North

Carolina, graduating in 1858 with honors. His college years exposed him to leading intellectual debates of the time, including heated discussions about states' rights and slavery that would soon tear the nation apart.

His ambitions led him to pursue legal studies at Cumberland University Law School in Tennessee, where he studied under Judge Nathan Green Sr., one of the South's most respected legal minds. After obtaining his degree in 1860, he returned to Columbus to establish his practice, focusing primarily on property law and civil disputes.

The outbreak of war in 1861 transformed Humphries from a promising young lawyer into a soldier. When Mississippi seceded on January 9, 1861, Humphries was among the first to volunteer. By 1862, he had received a lieutenant's commission in the Thirty-fifth Mississippi Infantry Regiment, Company K, known locally as the "Columbus Riflemen."

His military service included:

- Participation in the Vicksburg Campaign (1862-1863)

- Fighting at the Battle of Corinth (October 1862)
- Defense of Port Hudson (1863)
- Actions during the Atlanta Campaign (1864)

He rose to the rank of captain through demonstrated leadership and courage under fire. His wartime letters, some of which survive today, detail the harsh conditions of camp life, including disease outbreaks, food shortages, and the constant anxiety of impending battle.

After Appomattox, Humphries returned to a dramatically changed Columbus. Like many Confederate veterans, he took the requisite oath of allegiance to the Union and worked to rebuild his law practice, eventually entering the political arena. He specialized in helping fellow veterans navigate the complex legal landscape of Reconstruction.

He was also a prominent member of the local Columbus Chapter of the Ku Klux Klan under the leadership of former CSA Generals Jacob Sharp, Stephen D. Lee, and Jeptha Vining Harris. Humphries also served on the City Council from 1872-1876.

His fellow Mississippians elected him to the State Senate, where he served from 1880 to 1884, helping to shape policy during the challenging Reconstruction era. During his term, he served as Chairman of the Senate Judiciary Committee and championed tirelessly to create and fund the Industrial Institute and College for Women in Columbus.

Humphries' personal life reflected the complex social fabric of the post-war South. His 1871 marriage to Mary Thomas Jones, daughter of a prominent planter family, produced six children:

> William Washington III (1872)
> Thomas Gregory (1874)
> James Monroe (1876)
> Robert Lee (1878)
> Mary Elizabeth (1880)
> Benjamin Franklin (1883)

He purchased Riverview from Gilmer's widow in 1881. He and Mary lived there only a few short years before she contracted yellow fever and died. After Mary's death in 1885, he married Fannie Randall Moore in 1887, who helped raise his children and was a highly respected figure in Columbus society.

Humphries' health began declining in late 1903, possibly due to complications from old war wounds. The winter of 1904 proved particularly harsh, and on February 6th, he passed away at the age of 62 in his daughter's home on College Street. His funeral was one of the largest Columbus had seen, attended by Confederate veterans, political colleagues, and citizens from all walks of life. He was laid to rest in Friendship Cemetery in Columbus, the same city where his life's journey had begun. His grave, marked with his Confederate service record, stands as a testament to a life that spanned one of the most tumultuous periods in American history.

Humphries' life embodied the transformation of the American South: From antebellum prosperity to Civil War devastation through the challenges of Reconstruction and into the "New South" era of the late 19th century.

Riverview Parlor

The Young Humphries Brothers: A Tale of Tragic Destiny

T he dawn of the 20th century ushered in an era of unprecedented industrial growth across America, particularly in the South. Columbus, Mississippi, stood as a testament to this transformation – a bustling river town where steamboats churned the waters of the Tombigbee and locomotives thundered across iron bridges. The city, with its population of nearly 10,000, boasted newly installed electric streetlights, telephone lines, and the promise of modernity. The two sons of William W. Humphries, a bookkeeper by trade, would meet their fates in the very manifestations of industrial progress that defined their era – the railroad and the river.

Gregory Pegram Humphries cut an impressive figure in his Spanish-American War uniform, standing proudly among his fellow volunteers in Company D. His service record notes his participation in training exercises at Camp Pat

Henry, however the conflict ended before his unit could be deployed overseas. Upon his return, the railroad called to him, as it had to so many Humphries men before.

Gregory Pegram Humphries, born in 1877, followed in his grandfather's footsteps, taking up work as a railroad fireman for the M&O Railroad. As a fireman for the M&O Railroad, Gregory mastered the demanding art of maintaining steam pressure and managing the locomotive's voracious appetite for coal. His fellow workers remembered him as methodical and careful, often sharing coffee from his silver thermos during predawn shifts. He learned every click, hiss, and rumble of the mighty steam engines he tended.

The elder Humphries had dedicated over three decades to the same line, establishing a family legacy tied to the iron rails that crisscrossed the South. Gregory had already distinguished himself through service to his country in the Spanish-American War, proudly serving with Company D of the 2nd Mississippi Volunteers.

His younger brother, Henry Hart Humphries, born in 1881, lived in the shadow of the Tombigbee River, where the railroad bridge stretched across the rushing waters – a daily reminder of the intersection between progress and nature's power.

Henry Hart Humphries developed a deep connection to the Tombigbee River, fishing its banks and swimming its waters for countless hours. Local newspapers occasionally mentioned his swimming feats, including a notable rescue of a young boy who had fallen from a rowboat in the summer of 1907.

The tragic tale of the Humphries brothers unfolded in separate incidents, each equally devastating. In April 1905, on a Saturday night near midnight in Artesia, Mississippi, the explosion that claimed Gregory's life occurred on Engine No. 214, a relatively new Baldwin locomotive. Witnesses described a deafening blast that lit up the Artesia night like daybreak.

Gregory met his end in a violent locomotive explosion. The blast hurled him fifty feet backward from his position on the baggage car while scalding steam ensured his instant death. The cause of the explosion remained a mystery, with only the knowledge that the engine had been switching tracks at the time of the catastrophe.

The explosion that claimed Gregory's life occurred on Engine No. 214, a relatively new Baldwin locomotive. Witnesses described a deafening blast that lit up the Artesia night like daybreak. The investigation revealed that the locomotive's crown sheet had failed, though whether due to low water conditions or material defect remained disputed. The explosion left a crater in the railyard and scattered debris across three hundred feet.

On that fateful Sunday in 1909, Henry wore his best suit, having attended morning services at First Baptist Church. The railroad bridge where he met his end spanned 415 feet across the Tombigbee, its steel trusses rising 65 feet above the water. The bridge keeper, Thomas Morton, provided a detailed account of Henry's final moments, describing how he had called out "Help! Help!" three times before disappearing beneath the churning waters.

Henry's story would end in the swirling waters of the Tombigbee four years later. On what began as an ordinary Sunday morning, he left his home for what he described as a short walk. The railroad bridge, a familiar sight from his house, became the stage for his final moments. As a train approached, Henry stepped onto a middle pier to allow it safe passage. The bridge keeper, the sole witness to the tragedy, watched as Henry attempted to step back onto the bridge after the train passed, losing his balance and plummeting into the river below.

Despite being an accomplished swimmer, Henry faced insurmountable odds. The river, swollen and swift from recent rains, created treacherous conditions at what was already considered a dangerous section. In his final moments, Henry demonstrated remarkable composure, managing to shed his coat and call for help several times before the powerful current claimed him.

The Humphries brothers' stories serve as a poignant reminder of the price of progress in the American South, where the very engines of industrial advancement – the railroad and the river – claimed the lives of two young men from a single family, forever altering the course of their family's history.

The deaths of the Humphries brothers sent shockwaves through Columbus society. The Commercial Dispatch devoted front-page coverage to both tragedies and the brothers' funerals drew hundreds of mourners. Their deaths spurred safety improvements: the railroad implemented stricter boiler inspection protocols, while the bridge company installed additional safety platforms.

HUMPHRIES FUNERAL
HELD IN TUSKALOOSA.

Special to The Birmingham News.

TUSKALOOSA, Ala., April 10.—The remains of Gregory Humphries, who was killed by the explosion of an engine boiler at Artesia on Saturday were brought here yesterday for interment. The body was taken in charge at the depot by the local lodge of Brotherhood Locomotive Engineers and carried to the residence of John J. Neillson. The funeral services were held at 4 o'clock and the body was laid at rest in Evergreen cemetery.

The Birmingham News April !0, 1905 page 10.

A POPULAR YOUNG MAN DROWNED.

Mr. Henry H. Humphries Falls From the M. & O. Bridge Pier Last Sunday and is Drowned.

This community was profoundly shocked and his relatives and friends plunged into unspeakable grief by the sudden announcement of the drowning of Mr. Henry Humphries Sunday morning at half past ten o'clock. In the prime of a splendid and promising young manhood, holding positions of responsibility and trust in this city, beloved by a large circle of friends, who recognized in him one of the best and most exemplary types of our younger citizenship, possessing the esteem and confidence of everyone, his tragic end casts a shadow of gloom and sorrow over the city, from which it will take it a long time to recover.

Sunday morning Mr. Humphries, whose arduous duties as manager of the Central Gas House and Secretary and Treasurer of the Columbus Machinery Company, give little time or opportunity for recreation through the week, secured his little rifle and went toward the M. & O. bridge in search of pleasure. He had an engagement with friends to meet them at his office at the Machinery Co's. plant and while waiting for them he walked out on the Mobile & Ohio railroad bridge. He was in the center of the bridge when the south bound passenger train came along. He stepped off the track on to the middle pier of the structure and stood there until the train was nearly past him. His brothers, Messrs. Sam and Edward Humphries, were on the train and seeing them, Mr. Humphries waved to them. His brothers did not recognize him and it is thought that this salutation cost Mr. Humphries his life. In doing so he stepped back only a few inches and losing his balance fell backward into the raging river below. He left his little rifle on the pier as if to rid himself of every weight in the struggle for life which was to follow. The current at this point is very swift and the condition of the river, being high, made the waters all the more treacherous. Mr. Humphries was seen to strike the stream and disappear. A few seconds elapsed and he appeared some distance below the point where he fell. He raised his hands and cried to Mr. Joe Leon, keeper of the bridge, for help. He was a good swimmer and was sustaining himself admirably when his cries reached the ears of men on bank. When they saw him he was in the middle of the stream being carried rapidly down the stream. Gradually his swimming became weaker and he disappeared again below the murky waters of the Bigbee. A few seconds later his body was seen several feet below, again struggling in the water and then it disappeared and all was still.

Mr. Leon and others who were attracted by the cries for help rushed out on the bridge and saw the drowning man. They continually started towards the rescue, hoping that he would be enabled to breast the waters until they could reach him with a boat. Long before they were on the river however, Mr. Humphries was lost and they with hundreds of other friends immediately took on the work of recovering the body. The machinists who had worked for Mr. Humphries took up the work and their hammers were seen sounding at the forge as they made hooks and grappling irons to recover the body of the young man who had been so dear and kind to them. All day Sunday the river was dragged but without avail. The stream was greatly swollen, the channel was very deep, the current was strong and all of these efforts proved futile.

Monday and yesterday the workers in search of the body continued their ceaseless vigil, dragging the river where the drowning occurred, examining drifts as the waters receded, patrolling the banks for miles below this city and offering rewards to the people living along the river for the recovery of the body. The brothers of the deceased young men, Messrs Gregory and Sam Humphries, accompanied by friends secured two gasoline launches yesterday and went far down the river searching for the body and putting out patrols who will keep search on the same.

It will, in all probability be several days before the body is recovered. The water at this section is cold and it will, perhaps be longer than three days before it rises to the surface and then if it be in the current it may be carried down stream for many miles before it is recovered. The water is rapidly falling now and this fact leads the relatives and friends of the dead man to hope that it will greatly facilitate the recovery of his remains.

The Bigbee Hardware Company hired in Tuscaloosa for dynamite yesterday to use in the river in an attempt to recover the body and it is understood that it will probably be used today.

Henry H. Humphries was the third oldest son of the late Capt. W. W. Humphries of this city and he was one of Columbus' best known and most universally esteemed young men. Of fine mind and exemplary character he had taken a high position for one of his years in the commercial circles of this city and no young man had a larger circle of friends among all classes. He was beloved by the mechanics with whom his labors had fallen, he was beloved in the best social circles of this city in which he took such a prominent part and he was beloved by the older citizens of Columbus who recognized in him a straightforward, honest, manly young man, whose future held forth the promise of a useful and honorable career.

THE DISPATCH tenders its sincerest condolence and sympathy to the bereaved relatives and friends of the young man who so sudden death is a blow and a sorrow to all who knew him.

The Columbus Weekly Dispatch - Mar 02, 1905 · Page 3

67

The Origins of the Columbus Pilgrimage

In the late 1930s, as the United States was slowly emerging from the depths of the Great Depression, a group of visionary women in Columbus, Mississippi, embarked on a journey that would transform their city into a beacon of Southern history and hospitality. This is the story of the Columbus Pilgrimage, an event born out of necessity and nurtured by community spirit.

The story begins in 1937, when members of the Pioneer Club of Columbus made a pivotal journey to Natchez, Mississippi. There, they witnessed the success of the Natchez Garden Club Spring Pilgrimage, an event that showcased the town's antebellum homes and attracted tourists from far and wide. Inspired by what they saw, these women returned to Columbus with a vision: to create a similar event that would highlight their own city's rich architectural heritage.

In anticipation of their plans, the newly formed Galaxy Garden Club took a proactive step. They began planting wisteria vines along the highways leading into Columbus, setting the stage for what would become known as "The Pilgrimage of Wisteria Time in Columbus."

In 1939, an opportunity presented itself. The Mississippi Federation of Music Clubs announced that their annual convention would be held in Columbus in April 1940. Recognizing this as the perfect chance to launch their pilgrimage, a Columbus Pilgrimage Committee quickly formed.

The timing was both opportune and challenging. Like much of the nation, Columbus was still grappling with the effects of the Great Depression. Many of the grand antebellum homes, which would be the stars of the pilgrimage, had fallen into disrepair. Some had been divided into apartments as families struggled to keep their properties. Despite these obstacles, the committee pressed on, identifying over 25 potential homes for the tour.

Understanding the importance of publicity, the committee organized a special tour in the fall of 1939 for Associated Press travel writers. Among these journalists was the renowned Mississippi author Eudora Welty, an alumna of the local women's college. The resulting articles appeared in newspapers nationwide, from Memphis to New York, putting Columbus on the map as a destination for history enthusiasts.

The inaugural Columbus Spring Pilgrimage featured an impressive lineup of homes, including some that remain on the tour to this day: Camellia Place, Wisteria Place, Baskerville Manor, Snowdoun, Shadowlawn, Riverview, Colonnade, White Arches, and Waverly Mansion. These homes, along with others like Franklin Square, Rosewood Manor, and Temple Heights, offered visitors a glimpse into the grandeur of the antebellum South.

Interestingly, the descriptions of these homes by the early travel writers were limited by the architectural vocabulary of the time. Terms like "Gothic Revival" and "Italianate" were not commonly used in Southern architecture. This limitation in language led to some accidentally accurate descriptions of the earliest homes' late Federalist styling.

The Columbus Pilgrimage has since become an annual tradition, surviving through decades of change and challenge. It stands as a testament to the foresight of those early organizers and the enduring appeal of Southern history and hospitality.

Today, many of the homes that were part of that first tour in 1940 continue to welcome visitors, their doors opened by dedicated homeowners who share a passion for preserving and showcasing their city's rich architectural heritage. The Columbus Pilgrimage remains a vibrant celebration of history, community, and the enduring charm of the American South.

Photo of Riverview front porch *Life Magazine* March 8, 1943

About The Author

Patricia Shannon Evans is a local author, podcaster, and public historian. She is a fifth/sixth generation Mississippian. Her deep Southern roots and extensive family are rich with great characters and champion storytellers.

Evans attended Ole Miss, joined, a sorority and did all the things a "young lady" of the era was expected to do. But she chafed at going to dances, soirees, and teas. She was happiest either on the river or exploring an abandoned old homesite's cemetery. The world was her oyster, and she was eager for adventures.

She left soon after college, first for the Middle East and then Europe. Her three children (Taylor, Jenny, and Colin) claim their childhood was spent either sweating in a tent in tick and snake infested woods or freezing in castles and fortresses on wind and rainswept moors.

Evans returned home in the middle of Covid and earned an MFA in Creative Writing at Mississippi University for Women. She podcasts at *Tombigbee Tales* about local history old and new. She also posts a one-minute video on the Tombigbee Tales YouTube channel every day about people buried in Mississippi cemeteries (mostly Lowndes County).

Bibliography

Books and Monographs

1. Benjamin, Asher. *The American Builder's Companion*. New York: Dover Publications, Inc., 1969.

2. Crocker, Mary Wallace. *Historic Architecture in Mississippi*. Jackson, 1976.

3. Fricker, Jonathan, Donna Fricker, and Patricia L. Duncan. *Louisiana Architecture: A Handbook on Styles*. Lafayette, Louisiana: University of Southwestern Louisiana, The Center for Louisiana Studies, 1998.

4. Gamble, Robert. *The Alabama Catalog - Historic American Buildings Survey: A Guide to the Early Architecture of the State*. University of Alabama Press, 1987.

5. Hamlin, Talbot. *Greek Revival Architecture in America*. London, New York, Toronto: Oxford University Press, 1944.

6. P'Pool, Kenneth H. *Columbus: The Architectural History of a Mississippi Town,

1871-1866*. University Press of Mississippi, 1990 (unpublished manuscript).

7. Skates, John Ray. *Mississippi, A Bicentennial History*. New York: W.W. Norton and Company, Inc., 1979.

8. Smith, J. Frazer. *White Pillars-Early Life and Architecture of the Lower Mississippi Valley Country*. New York: Bramhall House, 1941.

Academic Journal Articles
1. Fields, Cameron L. "Equity Law Consequences upon the Mississippi Married Women's Property Act of 1839." *Journal of Mississippi History*, Vol. 77, No. 1, 2015.